This book belongs to ...

....

OXFORD
UNIVERSITY PRESS

Great Clarendon Street, Oxford, OX2 6DP,
United Kingdom

Oxford University Press is a department of the University of Oxford.
It furthers the University's objective of excellence in research, scholarship,
and education by publishing worldwide. Oxford is a registered trade mark of
Oxford University Press in the UK and in certain other countries

*Seasick, Craig Saves the Day, Hungry Floppy,
Looking After Gran* text © Roderick Hunt 2005, 2007, 2008
Hungry Floppy, Looking After Gran illustrations © Alex Brychta 2005
Seasick, Craig Saves the Day illustrations © Alex Brychta and Nick Schon 2007, 2008

ISBN: 978-0-19-273436-5

3 5 7 9 10 8 6 4 2

Typeset in Edbaskerville

Paper used in the production of this book is a natural, recyclable product made
from wood grown in sustainable forests. The manufacturing process conforms
to the environmental regulations of the country of origin.

Acknowledgements;
Series Editors: Kate Ruttle, Annemarie Young

READ WITH
Biff,
Chip &
Kipper

Looking After Gran
and Other Stories

OXFORD
UNIVERSITY PRESS

Tips for Reading Together

Children learn best when learning is fun.

- Talk about the title and the picture on the cover.
- Identify the letter patterns *ea*, *ee* and *y* and talk about the sound (phoneme) they make when you read them.
- Look at the *ea*, *ee* and *y* words on page 4. Say each word and then say the sounds in each word (e.g. *seat*, *s-ea-t*; *feet*, *f-ee-t*; *sandy*, *s-a-n-d-y*).
- Read the story and find the words with *ea* and *ee*.
- Do the fun activity at the end of the book.

Children enjoy re-reading stories and this helps to build their confidence.

Have fun!

After you have read the story, find all of the hats in the pictures.

The main sound practised in this book is 'ee' as in *beach*, *cheese* and *jelly*.

For more hints and tips on helping your child become a successful and enthusiatic reader look at our website www.oxfordowl.co.uk.

Seasick

Written by Roderick Hunt
Illustrated by Nick Schon,
based on the original characters
created by Roderick Hunt and Alex Brychta

OXFORD
UNIVERSITY PRESS

Say the sound and read the words

ee

- see
- cheese
- feet
- feel

ea

- sea
- beach
- seat
- cream

y

funny

jetty

jolly

sandy

9

Gran had a hut, by the sea.

"It's my beach hut," said Gran.

"I call it Sandy Feet," she said.

Gran had six seats in the hut.

They had a picnic.

"Cheese rolls," said Gran. "Then jelly and cream."

"What a picnic," said Biff.

"It's a feast."

Gran had a boat at the jetty.

"I call it Jolly Jean," she said.

It was fun in Jolly Jean.

"I can see a seal," said Chip.

But then the sea was choppy.
The boat went up and down.

"My tummy feels funny,"
said Wilma.

"Sorry," said Gran. "We had too
much jelly and cream."

They went back to the beach hut.

"Beans on toast?" said Gran.

Talk about the story

29

Word jumble

Make the *ee*, *ea* and *y* words from the story.

ch b ea

ll j y e

ch ea

ch pp o y

l ee f

ea s f t

e y j tt

ee s

ea s t

ee, ea or y?

The sound 'ee' can be spelled *ee*, *ea* and *y*. Match the right 'ee' spelling to the pictures and complete the word.

s___

Joll_ J___n

b___ns

ch___se

s___l

f___t

33

Find the *ea* words

Read the words. Point to the ones you can find
in the picture.

beach   beans   feast   Jolly Jean

sea   seal   seasick   seat

Tips for Reading Together

Children learn best when reading is fun.

- Talk about the title and the picture on the front cover.

- Identify the letter patterns *ai*, *a-e* and *ay* in the title and talk about the sound they make when you read them ('ai').

- Look at the *ai*, *a-e* and *ay* words on page 4. Say the sounds in each word and then say the word (e.g. *w-ai-t, wait; r-a-c-e, race; s-t-ay, stay*).

- Read the story then find the words with *ai*, *a-e* and *ay*.

- Talk about the story and do the fun activity at the end of the book.

Children enjoy re-reading stories and this helps to build their confidence.

After you have read the story, play Kim's Game on page 12. How many objects can you remember?

The main sound practised in this book is 'ai' as in *Craig, day, game.*

For more hints and tips on helping your child become a successful and enthusiastic reader look at our website www.oxfordowl.co.uk.

Craig Saves the Day

Written by Roderick Hunt
Illustrated by Nick Schon,
based on the original characters
created by Roderick Hunt and Alex Brychta

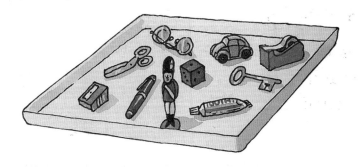

OXFORD
UNIVERSITY PRESS

Say the sound and read the words

ai

Gail

w**ai**t

t**ai**ls

Cr**ai**g

ay

d**ay**

hoor**ay**

st**ay**

pl**ay**

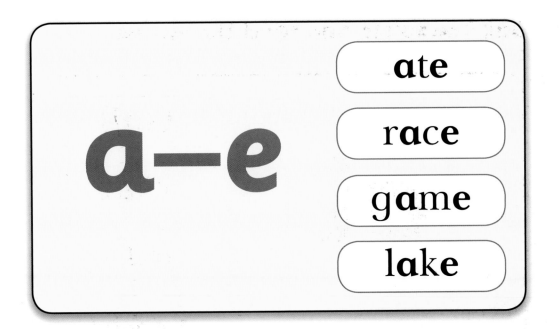

a–e

- ate
- race
- game
- lake

39

"So this is Haygate Lake,"
said Chip.

Gail was the leader.

"Wait for Craig," she said.

"Let Chip push me," said Craig.

"It's a fun day with games and races," said Gail.

"You stay in the same team
all day," she said.

Wilf, Chip and Craig were in the red team.

They played a game called 'Tails', but the green team won.

They played 'Kim's Game'. Craig
was good at it.

"Hooray," yelled Chip.
"We won. The red team won."

It was time to eat.
Wilf had a cake.

50

He gave it to Gail and they all
ate some.

They had an egg and spoon race.
The green team won.

They had a pea race and Craig won it.

The last game was a boat race.

Craig won the race.

"Good for Craig," said Chip.

Talk about the story

Where did the scouts go on their day out?

What was the first game they played?

What is Kim's Game? Have you played it?

ai, ay or a-e?

The sound 'ai' can be spelled *ay, ai* and *a-e*. Match the right 'ai' spelling to the pictures and complete the word.

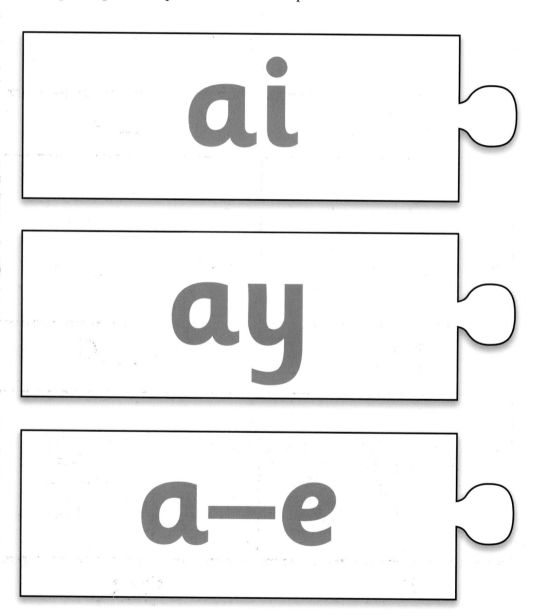

g_m_

r__n

pl__

Cr__g

tr__

g_t_

Picture puzzle

Find as many *ai*,
ay and *a–e* words as
you can in the picture.

ai

 **ay**

 a-e

Answers: Craig, Gail, Haygate Lake, cake, plate

63

Jumbled letters

Make the *ai*, *ay* and *a–e* words from the story.

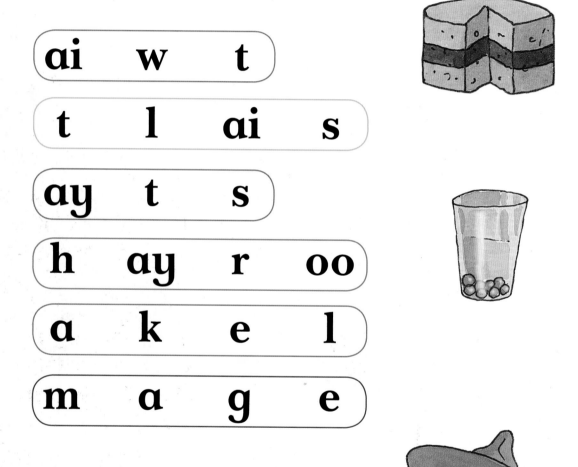

ai   w   t

t   l   ai   s

ay   t   s

h   ay   r   oo

a   k   e   l

m   a   g   e

Tips for Reading Together

Children learn best when reading is fun.

- Talk about the title and the picture on the front cover.

- Discuss what you think the story might be about.

- Read the story together, inviting your child to read as much of it as they can.

- Give lots of praise as your child reads, and help them when necessary.

- If they get stuck, try reading the first sound of the word, or break the word into chunks, or read the whole sentence again. Focus on the meaning.

- Re-read the story later, encouraging your child to read as much of it as they can.

Children enjoy re-reading stories and this helps to build their confidence.

Have fun!

After you have read the story, find the letters in the pictures that make up the name GOLDILOCKS.

This book includes these useful common words:
thought   very   so   away

For more hints and tips on helping your child become a successful and enthusiastic reader look at our website www.oxfordowl.co.uk.

Hungry Floppy

Written by Roderick Hunt
Illustrated by Alex Brychta

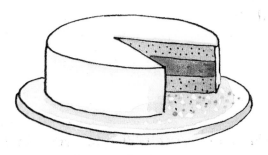

OXFORD
UNIVERSITY PRESS

The family went camping. They
put up a tent.

It took a long time to put up the
tent. Floppy was hungry.

Floppy was so hungry, he ran
off to look for food.

A man was cooking.

"That smells good," thought Floppy,

"and I'm so hungry."

"Go away!" called the man.
"You can't have our dinner."
Floppy ran off.

Floppy saw a dog's bowl.
"This smells good," he thought,
"and I'm so hungry."

A big dog barked at Floppy.
"Go away," growled the dog.
"You can't have my dinner."

Floppy was lost. He saw lots
of tents but they all looked
the same to him.

Floppy could smell something.
He sniffed and sniffed. Something
smelled good.

Floppy went inside the tent.
He saw three plates. There was a
slice of cake on each one.

By now, Floppy was *very* hungry.
So he ate the big slice.

He was still hungry, so he ate the
smaller slice.

But Floppy was *still* hungry, so
he ate the very small slice, too.
"I need a rest now," he thought.

There were three beds. Floppy
lay on the blue bed, but it was
too hard.

Then Floppy lay on the green
bed, but it was too soft.

In the end, he lay on the red bed.
It was not too hard or too soft. It
was just right. So he went to sleep.

Soon, a girl came back to the
tent with her mum and dad.
It was Anneena!

"Someone has eaten my cake,"
said Anneena.

"Someone has eaten *all* the cake," said Anneena's mum. "And look who's sleeping on your bed."

"It's Floppy!" said Anneena. "What are you doing here, you naughty dog?"

Anneena and her dad looked
for Biff and Chip. At last, they
found them.

"What a surprise to see you!"
said Biff.

Anneena told them about Floppy.

"Never mind," said Dad. "Stay
and have some of our cake."

Talk about the story

Why did Floppy steal the food? Was he wrong to steal it?

Why didn't Floppy go and look for Biff and Chip himself?

How is this story like Goldilocks and the Three Bears?

What would you do if you got lost in a strange place?

Matching pairs

Find pairs of things that start with the same letter.
Which one isn't in the story?

Tips for Reading Together

Children learn best when reading is fun.

- Talk about the title and the picture on the front cover.
- Discuss what you think the story might be about.
- Read the story together, inviting your child to read as much of it as they can.
- Give lots of praise as your child reads, and help them when necessary.
- If they get stuck, try reading the first sound of the word, or break the word into chunks, or read the whole sentence again. Focus on the meaning.
- Re-read the story later, encouraging your child to read as much of it as they can.

Children enjoy re-reading stories and this helps to build their confidence.

Have fun!

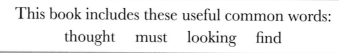

After you have read the story, find the 10 even numbers hidden in the pictures.

This book includes these useful common words:
thought   must   looking   find

For more hints and tips on helping your child become a successful and enthusiastic reader look at our website www.oxfordowl.co.uk.

Looking
After Gran

Written by Roderick Hunt
Illustrated by Alex Brychta

OXFORD
UNIVERSITY PRESS

98

The family was going away.

"Look after Floppy," said Dad.

Gran liked looking after Floppy.

She took him for lots of walks.

She threw sticks for him to
chase and balls for him to catch.

Gran had a motorbike.

It was bright red.

"Jump in, Floppy," said Gran.

Gran put on her crash helmet.

"Where are we going?"

thought Floppy.

Soon, they were zooming
into town.

"Isn't this fun!" said Gran.

"Not for me!" thought Floppy.

At last, Gran stopped. She parked
the motorbike on the sand.

"Stay here, Floppy," said Gran.
"Look after the motorbike. I'm
going shopping."

Gran was away for a long time.
The tide started to come in. A wave
splashed the front wheel.

Then a wave splashed the
back wheel.

"Gran has parked too close
to the sea!" thought Floppy.

"I must find Gran," thought
Floppy.

He ran into the town as fast
as he could.

Sniff! Sniff! went Floppy.
He could tell where Gran
had been. She had been in the
butcher's shop.

"Yum! Bones," thought Floppy.

"Get out!" yelled the butcher. "No dogs in here!"

Floppy ran back into
the street.

"I must find Gran," he
thought.

Sniff! Sniff! went Floppy.

Gran had been in the bread shop.

"Get out!" yelled the baker. "No dogs in here!"

Floppy ran back into
the street.

"I must find Gran,"
he thought.

Then Floppy saw Gran.

She was in the hat shop.

Floppy ran in and barked.

"Get out!" said the lady. "No dogs
in here!"

"Come on, Gran!" thought Floppy.

Floppy ran out of the shop.

Gran ran after him.

"Come back!" called the lady.

"You haven't paid for that hat."

Floppy ran
back to the beach.
Gran puffed
after him.

"Oh no! My motorbike,"
shouted Gran.

She ran into the sea and pushed
her motorbike out.

"Well done, Floppy," said Gran.
"You saved my motorbike!"

Gran spoke to Mum.

"I'm not looking after Floppy,"
she said. "He's looking after me!"

Talk about the story

Why didn't Floppy like going on Gran's motorbike?

Why did Gran leave Floppy with her motorbike?

Gran told Floppy to stay. Why was he right not to stay?

What animal would you like to look after for a day?

Spot the difference

Find the ten differences on the motorbikes.

Read with Biff, Chip and Kipper
The UK's best-selling home reading series

Phonics

First Stories

	Phonics	First Stories
Level 1 Getting ready to read		
Level 2 Starting to read		
Level 3 Becoming a reader		
Level 4 Developing as a reader		
Level 5 Building confidence in reading		
Level 6 Reading with confidence		

Phonics stories help children practise their sounds and letters, as they learn to do in school.

First Stories have been specially written to provide practice in reading everyday language.

Read with Biff, Chip and Kipper Collections:

2 Phonics and 2 First Stories in every collection

 Up You Go and Other Stories

 Six in a Bed and Other Stories

 Funny Fish and Other Stories

 The Fizz-Buzz and Other Stories

 Floppy and the Bone and Other Stories

 I Can Trick a Tiger and Other Stories

 The Moon Jet and Other Stories

 Dragon Danger and Other Stories

 Husky Adventure and Other Stories

 Looking After Gran and Other Stories

 Hairy-Scary Monster and Other Stories

Secret of the Sands and Other Stories

Phonics support

Flashcards are a really fun way to practise phonics and build reading skills. Age 3+

My Phonics Kit is designed to support you and your child as you practise phonics together at home. It includes stickers, workbooks, interactive eBooks, support for parents and more! Age 5+

Read Write Inc. Phonics: A range of fun rhyming stories to support decoding skills. Age 4+

Songbirds Phonics: Lively and engaging phonics stories from Children's Laureate, Julia Donaldson. Age 4+

Help your child's reading with essential tips, advice on phonics and free eBooks
www.oxfordowl.co.uk